USBORNE FIRST NATURE BOOKS

TREES

Designed by
David Bennett

Illustrated by
Bob Bampton *(The Garden Studio)*
Wendy Bramall *(Artist Partners)*
Paul Brooks *(John Martin Artists)*
Frankie Coventry *(Artist Partners)*
Sarah Fox-Davies · Mick Loates *(The Garden Studio)*
Andy Martin · Dee McLean *(Linden Artists)*
David More *(Linden Artists)* · Ralph Stobart
Sally Voke *(Middletons)* · James Woods *(Middletons)*

Language Consultant
Betty Root

Consultant Editor
Esmond Harris *B.Sc., Dip.For., F.I.For.,*
Director of the Royal Forestry Society
of England, Wales and Northern Ireland.

Cover design by Amanda Barlow
Cover illustration by Isabel Bowring *(The Gallery)*

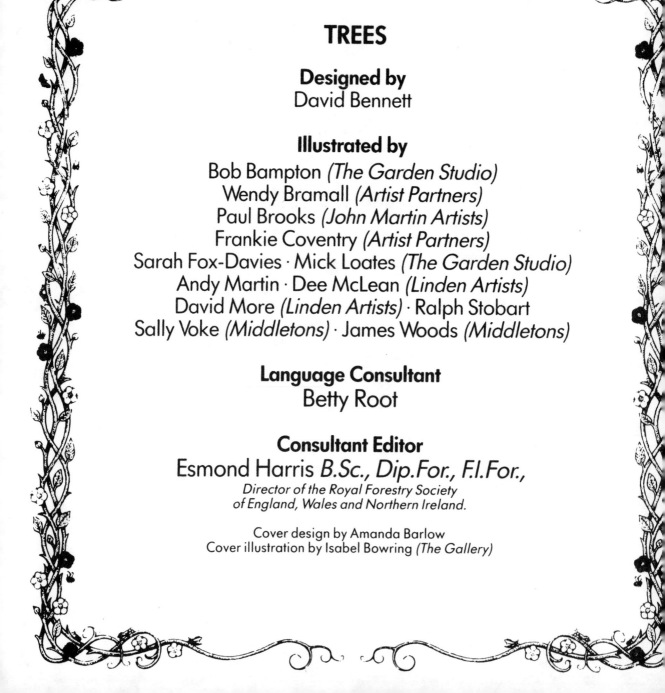

USBORNE FIRST NATURE
TREES

RUTH THOMSON

Games in this book

1. Hunt the Nut Weevil

Nut Weevils live on trees. Can you find 10 more Nut Weevils in this book?

2. Watch the leaf bud open

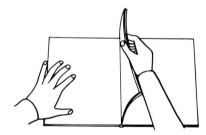

Hold the book like this.

Watch the top right hand corner and flick the pages over fast.

watch here

Amazing facts about trees

Trees are the largest plants in the world. They also live the longest.

On a warm day in spring, a large tree like this takes up 250 gallons of water from the soil. The water would fill five baths.

Trees cover about one third of the earth's surface.

Sometimes, the roots of a tree spread wider than its branches.

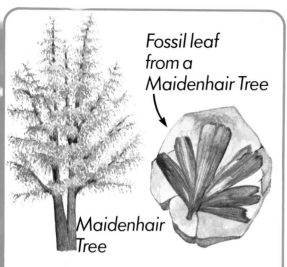

Fossil leaf from a Maidenhair Tree

Maidenhair Tree

Maidenhair trees today look almost the same as ones that grew 200 million years ago.

Bristlecone Pine Tree

This tree has been alive for 4,900 years. It grows in America.

People say that this tree has enough wood to make all these bungalows. It is the biggest tree in the world. It is 83 metres tall and 24 metres round the trunk.

This Sierra Redwood tree grows in California, in North America.

3

Trees in the countryside

This picture shows you some of the places where trees grow. Some of them grow naturally and some are planted by people.

This is a windy hillside. The branches of the trees grow bent over because of the wind.

Trees in a wood grow close together. They have thin trunks and not very many lower branches.

People sometimes plant trees around their houses to protect them from wind and frost.

A tree growing on its own has spreading branches.

Some trees grow near water.

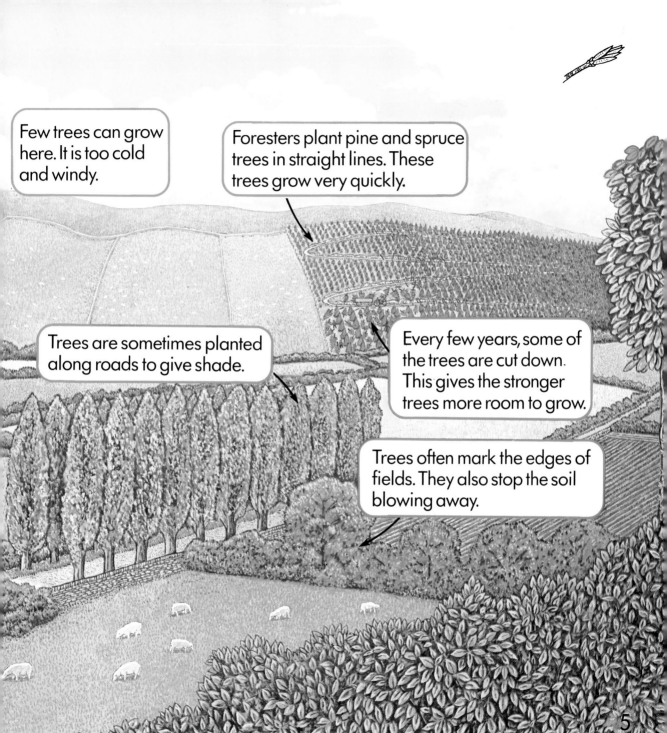

Few trees can grow here. It is too cold and windy.

Foresters plant pine and spruce trees in straight lines. These trees grow very quickly.

Trees are sometimes planted along roads to give shade.

Every few years, some of the trees are cut down. This gives the stronger trees more room to grow.

Trees often mark the edges of fields. They also stop the soil blowing away.

5

Under the ground

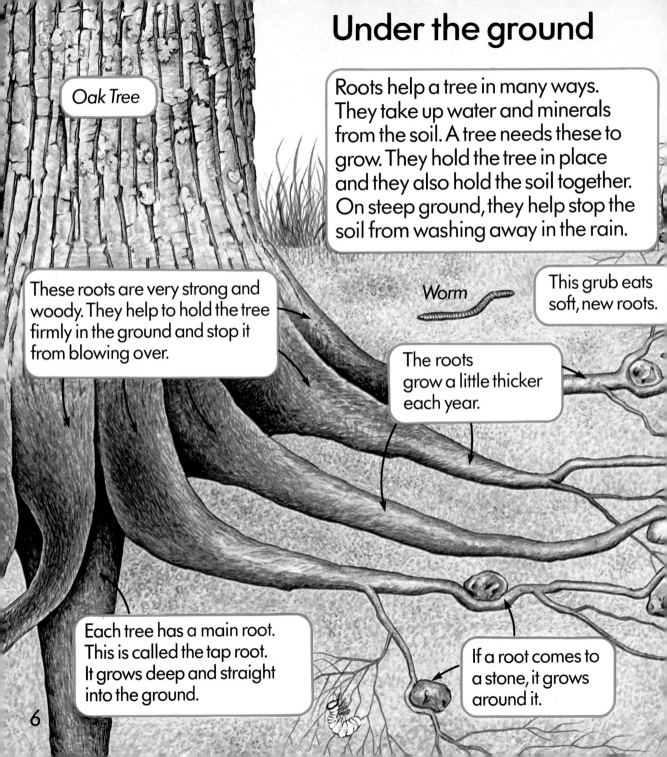

Oak Tree

Roots help a tree in many ways. They take up water and minerals from the soil. A tree needs these to grow. They hold the tree in place and they also hold the soil together. On steep ground, they help stop the soil from washing away in the rain.

Worm

This grub eats soft, new roots.

These roots are very strong and woody. They help to hold the tree firmly in the ground and stop it from blowing over.

The roots grow a little thicker each year.

Each tree has a main root. This is called the tap root. It grows deep and straight into the ground.

If a root comes to a stone, it grows around it.

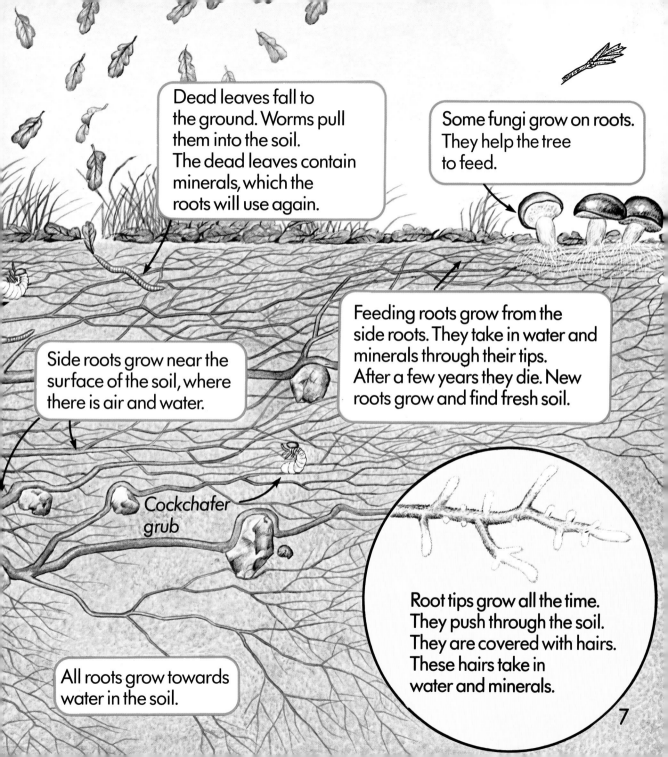

Dead leaves fall to the ground. Worms pull them into the soil. The dead leaves contain minerals, which the roots will use again.

Some fungi grow on roots. They help the tree to feed.

Side roots grow near the surface of the soil, where there is air and water.

Feeding roots grow from the side roots. They take in water and minerals through their tips. After a few years they die. New roots grow and find fresh soil.

Cockchafer grub

Root tips grow all the time. They push through the soil. They are covered with hairs. These hairs take in water and minerals.

All roots grow towards water in the soil.

7

How a twig grows

This is how a Beech twig grows in one year.

This is the leading bud. It is covered with scales that protect it. The new stem and leaves are inside the scales.

These are side buds.

1. Winter

The new stem grows and the leaves unfold. The scales are pushed apart.

The side buds grow into side shoots.

The new leaves are soft and pale.

2. Spring

3. Summer

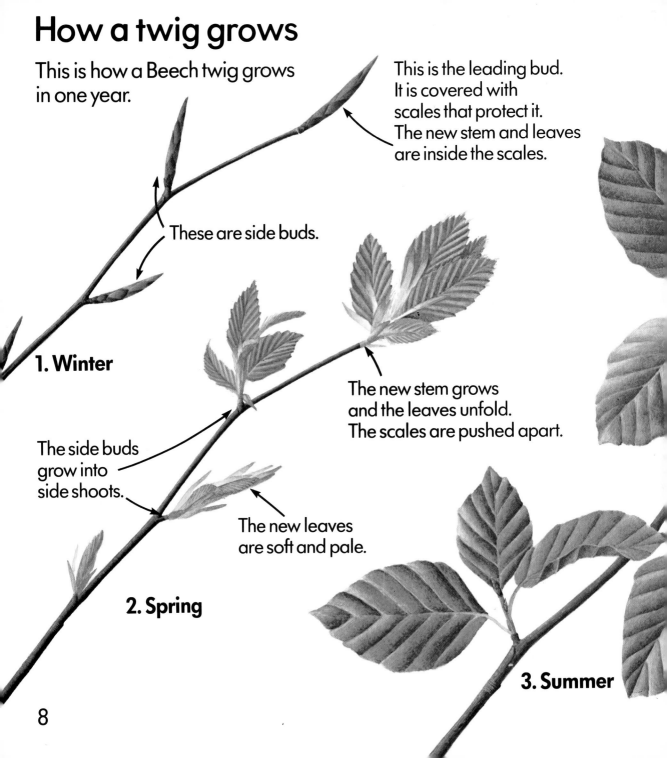

8

By summer, the stems are stiff and the leaves are dark green and shiny.

When the twig stops growing, it makes a new leading bud. Next spring, this bud will grow into a new shoot.

Towards the end of summer, a new bud is made just above each leaf stalk. Next year, this bud will grow into a new side shoot.

The leaves turn brown before they fall off.

This is where the leading bud was in the winter. The bud scales have left a scar. It is called a girdle scar. If you count the girdle scars on a twig, you can find out how old the twig is. This twig is two years old.

4. Autumn

9

Tree stumps

This is the inside of a healthy tree stump.

Most of the inside is sapwood. This carries water and minerals up from the roots to the leaves.

A very thin layer under the bark makes a new ring of sapwood every year.

In the middle is the heartwood. It is old, dead sapwood. It is very hard and strong.

Bark stops the tree from drying out and protects it from insects and disease. Bark cannot stretch. It splits or peels as the wood inside grows. New bark grows underneath.

This is how a tree may die.

spores

Fungus spores in the air get into a wound in the tree.

The fungus spreads inside the trunk. The heartwood rots.

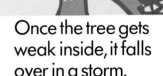

The heartwood in this tree is rotten.

Once the tree gets weak inside, it falls over in a storm.

When a tree dies, the bark becomes loose.
Animals and plants can get under the bark.
Many of them feed on the rotting wood.

Bracket Fungi grow on the trunk and feed on the rotting wood.

Slugs eat dead leaves and fungi. In dry weather they hide in cracks under the bark.

Longhorn Beetle

Scarlet Cup Fungi

Centipedes live under the bark. They come out at night to hunt for small insects.

Bark Beetles and their grubs make long tunnels under the bark.

Woodlice hide in damp places under the bark. They feed on rotting wood.

Millipedes live on the ground. They feed on dead leaves.

11

Deciduous tree leaves

Many trees are deciduous. This means that they lose their leaves in autumn. Most deciduous trees have soft, flat leaves.

Lime trees lose their leaves in autumn.

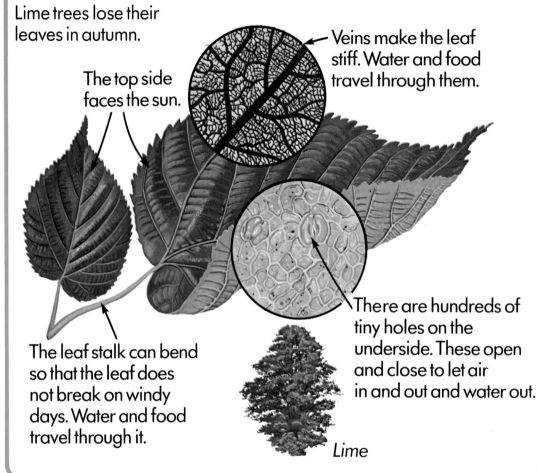

The top side faces the sun.

Veins make the leaf stiff. Water and food travel through them.

The leaf stalk can bend so that the leaf does not break on windy days. Water and food travel through it.

There are hundreds of tiny holes on the underside. These open and close to let air in and out and water out.

Rowan

Oak

Lime

Sycamore

Quaking Aspen

Horse Chestnut

Evergreen tree leaves

Other trees are called evergreens.
They keep their leaves all winter.
Most evergreens have tough, waxy leaves.

Pine trees have evergreen leaves.
Pine leaves are long and narrow.
They can stay alive in winter
because they are tough and
thick. Their waxy skin
stops them from drying
out. They can still make
some food in winter.

The veins
are in
lines.

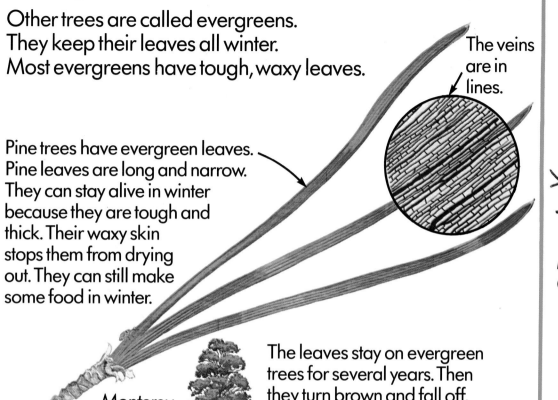

Monterey Pine

The leaves stay on evergreen
trees for several years. Then
they turn brown and fall off.
They do not fall off all at
once, so the tree always has
some leaves.

Italian Cypress

Snow Gum

Leaves are many different shapes, but they all do the same
work. Turn over the page to see what they do.

Norway Spruce

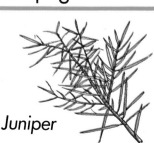

Juniper

Evergreen Oak

Scots Pine

What leaves do

A tree breathes and feeds with its leaves.
Follow the numbers to see how a tree makes its food.

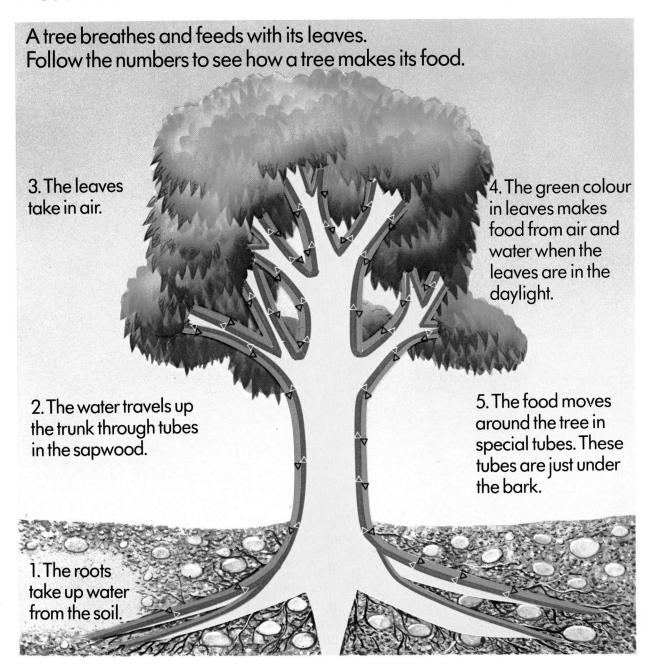

3. The leaves take in air.

4. The green colour in leaves makes food from air and water when the leaves are in the daylight.

2. The water travels up the trunk through tubes in the sapwood.

5. The food moves around the tree in special tubes. These tubes are just under the bark.

1. The roots take up water from the soil.

Why do deciduous trees lose their leaves in autumn?

Silver Maple

The corky layer forms here.

1. In autumn, it is not warm enough for leaves to make much food. Also, wind and cold weather would damage soft leaves.

2. A corky layer grows across the leaf stalk. Water cannot get to the leaf any more. The leaf changes colour.

This is the new leaf bud. Below it is the scar where the leaf was joined to the twig.

3. The leaf dries out and dies. The wind blows it off the tree.

4. All the leaves fall off. The tree rests until spring.

Tree flowers

All trees have flowers. Flowers have stamens, which hold pollen, and a pistil, which holds ovules. Pollen that lands on the top of the pistil grows down to join with the ovules. This is called fertilization. Fertilized ovules grow into seeds.

1. The petals and sweet scent attract insects. The insects feed on a sweet liquid inside the flower. This is called nectar.

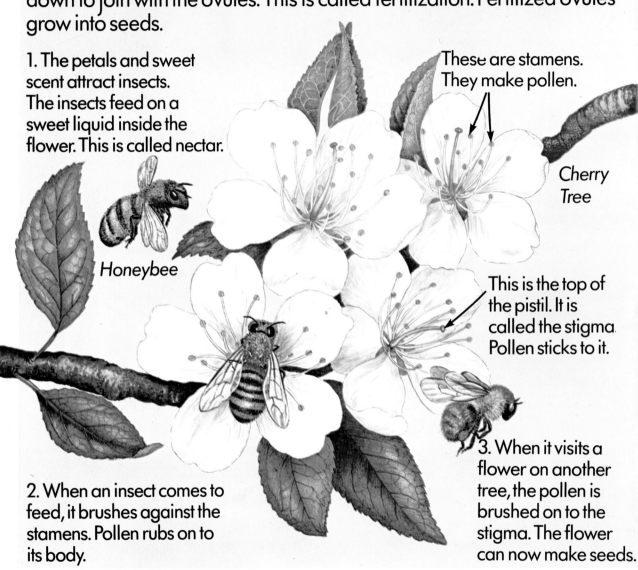

These are stamens. They make pollen.

Cherry Tree

Honeybee

This is the top of the pistil. It is called the stigma. Pollen sticks to it.

2. When an insect comes to feed, it brushes against the stamens. Pollen rubs on to its body.

3. When it visits a flower on another tree, the pollen is brushed on to the stigma. The flower can now make seeds.

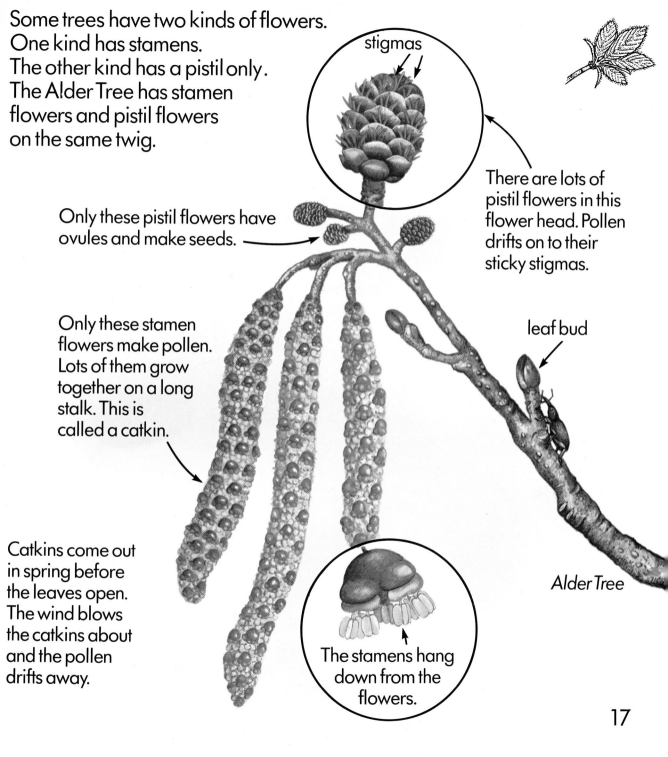

Some trees have two kinds of flowers.
One kind has stamens.
The other kind has a pistil only.
The Alder Tree has stamen
flowers and pistil flowers
on the same twig.

stigmas

There are lots of
pistil flowers in this
flower head. Pollen
drifts on to their
sticky stigmas.

Only these pistil flowers have
ovules and make seeds.

Only these stamen
flowers make pollen.
Lots of them grow
together on a long
stalk. This is
called a catkin.

leaf bud

Catkins come out
in spring before
the leaves open.
The wind blows
the catkins about
and the pollen
drifts away.

Alder Tree

The stamens hang
down from the
flowers.

17

Fruits and seeds

The fertilized ovules grow into seeds. Fruits grow to hold and protect them.

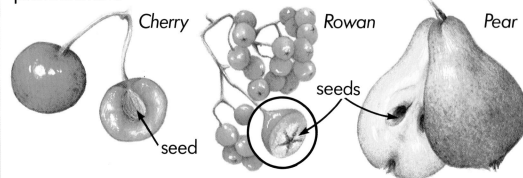

Cherry

Rowan

Pear

seeds

seed

These fruits are soft and juicy. Birds and animals eat them. Some have only one seed inside, others have lots.

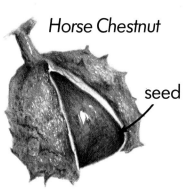

Horse Chestnut

seed

This fruit is spiky. It protects the seed inside.

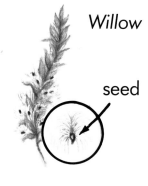

Willow

seed

This fruit is made of lots of seeds with feathery tops.

Hornbeam

Seed is in here

wing

This fruit is hard and dry. It has a leafy wing.

Sitka Spruce

Lime

Plane

Birch

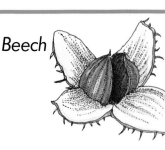

Beech

Hazel

Many evergreen trees have fruits called cones. The flowers that grow at the tips of new shoots grow into cones. Sometimes this takes two years.

Pine flowers are made up of soft scales. Each scale has two ovules inside. When pollen lands on the ovules they start to change into seeds. The scales close up to protect the seeds.

ovules

A Pine flower cut in half

Pine flower

Yew

This cone is a year old. The seeds inside are not ripe yet. The scales are hard and tightly shut.

Juniper

This cone is two years old. It is large and woody. The seeds inside are ripe. On a dry day, the scales open and the seeds fall out.

Scots Pine

seeds

Crab Apple

Mulberry

Sweet Chestnut

Black Locust

19

How seeds are moved

When the seeds in the fruits are ripe, the wind or animals may move them away from the tree. There is not enough light under the parent tree for the seedlings to grow well.

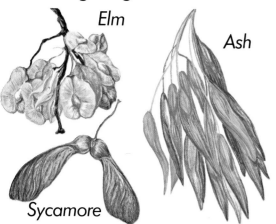

Elm

Ash

Sycamore

Fruits with wings spin away from the tree.

Plane

White Poplar

Some fruits are very light. They have tiny hairs that help them float away in the wind.

acorn

Oak Tree

Squirrels carry acorns away from Oak Trees and bury them. Birds feed on acorns and drop some. A few of the acorns grow into trees.

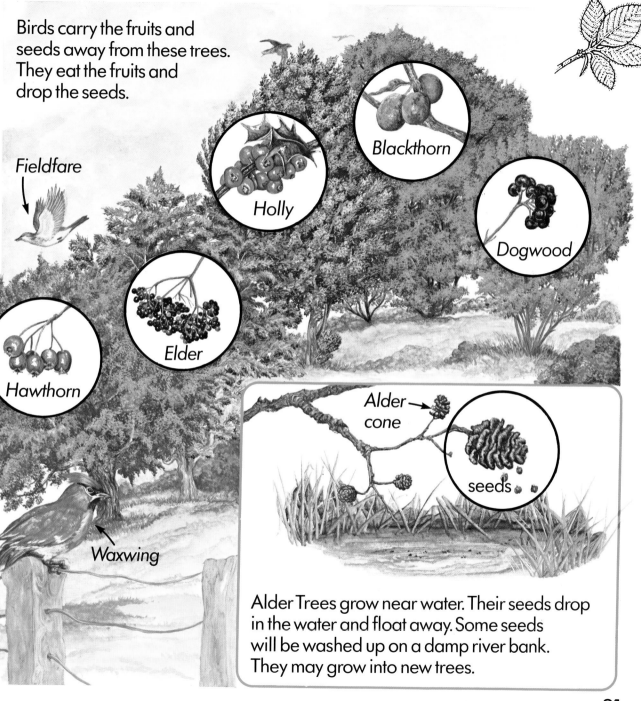

Birds carry the fruits and seeds away from these trees. They eat the fruits and drop the seeds.

Fieldfare

Holly

Blackthorn

Dogwood

Elder

Hawthorn

Waxwing

Alder cone

seeds

Alder Trees grow near water. Their seeds drop in the water and float away. Some seeds will be washed up on a damp river bank. They may grow into new trees.

Life on a tree

Keep a record book about a tree.
See how many insects live on the leaves or rest on the bark.
Watch how many birds visit it. Notice if any plants grow on it.

JUNE

I saw these willow fruits.

JUNE

I found a weevil on a leaf.

When I touched it, it folded its legs.

Herald Moth caterpillar

Some caterpillars are difficult to spot. Search carefully for them.

Dragonfly

Flying insects sometimes rest on the leaves in summer.

Willow fruits

Look for Willow fruits in spring and summer.

Poplar Hawk Moth

Some moths rest on the trunk in the day. They fly at night.

White Willow

Leaf Beetle

Look for beetles on the leaves and flowers.

Birds often visit trees to nest or sleep. Some search for seeds or insects.

Red Underwing Moth

These animals live on Willow trees. Willow trees often grow in wet places.

23

Picture puzzle

People eat many things that grow on trees. They make many things from the wood. There are at least 20 things in this picture that come from trees. How many can you find?

INDEX

TREES